ISBN 979-8-9913942-6-0

Published by Hidden Hand Press
www.hiddenhandbooks.com

HIDDEN HAND PRESS

OR MAYBE WE JUST SPENT OUR WHOLE LIVES DYING

by John Sweet

TABLE OF CONTENTS

PART I: all pain should be someone else's fault

PART II: the house on fire becomes the palace of ashes

PART III: how much of yr pointless pain are you willing to blame on everyone else?

PART I:

all pain should be someone else's fault

SONG

getting old, motherfucker

addicted to thoughts of
suicide, to internet porn, and one
doesn't need to preclude
the other.

every day can still be the
beginning of the end.

and did you waste 25 years in this
little slice of nowhere
thinking the future might find you?

were you drunk, maybe
messed up on crank, maybe busy
sleeping with your girlfriend's younger sister?

1

and you get married at some point,

have kids—

get divorced,

get bitter,

forget how to swim,

close your eyes and

touch bottom.

CITY OF MASKS

digging for the bones of
all the great surrealists beneath the
bitter winter sun but we were
too far away from mexico for
our voices to be heard.

we believed and
then we believe.

hope is a wheel but the
earth remains flat and so we
build machines that have a need for god.

we build a god less efficient than
our faultiest machines,

construct delicate songbirds from
rusted wire and scraps of tin and we
write out our pain for others to ignore.

i scratch the names of lesser saints
across yr lover's naked back and
she begs for more.

she understands the strength
within pain,

she opens her heart to the joy
that comes from suffering.

explains how the decision between
dead and lonely
needs to be made every day but
at the crucial moment
i am a coward

in the last bloodless light of day—
i am a vampire.

you gotta be willing to walk a
very long way before you find someone
willing to give a shit about your pain.

GREY-EYED DREAMER

and in the frozen sunlight, we are
burning every bastard god and all of
their false prophets and
we are hungry out here but
not yet crippled.

we are liars but
never alone.

and it hurts growing old and
it matters that you care
but it's inevitable that every truth we find
will end up lost again.

it's the song on the radio and
it's the stranger's body found out
by the railroad tracks.

it's your fate to be crushed by the landslide and

then it's mine to be crucified by the zealots, and the

air we breathe in this bitter house is

bright blue and luminous and as

beautiful as any poison.

the poems I write for you are

the ones that pin me to the floor;

the mercy you show me is something i

would never think to offer myself.

the source of every river of blood

is always the

heart of the weakest child.

IN THE CLEAR BLUE LIGHT OF THE
EVERYDAY

you are not the
dead man i dreamt of but
    you are the same and
        he is the father.

this is the house but
we are not the owners.

indifferent paintings on
cracked and peeling walls.

indifferent poet at a
chipped and scarred desk says
he doesn't expect you to

understand his pain.

asks for a drink

a cigarette

a light

but his wife's closet is empty—

we are all in love with

the wrong truths.

some clueless asshole tells you

you're a god and you choose to

believe him and now the

whole weekend is fucked.

the whole month is ruined.

a cheap motel room at

the city's edge:

free HBO and a view of the
interstate and it's here that i
finally realize what a serious
business hating yourself really is.

poet's wife asks for a drink
                    for a cigarette
                    or a light but
i need to get back home.

the children no longer trust me
when i tell them I love them.

the pictures they draw hang crooked
on smudged and faded walls,
the ghosts refuse to fade even in
                    the brutal light of day.

all i'm asking from you is
some small amount of belief and
all i'm saying is that you're
not the dead man.

this is his house,
but the mother is crying:

says she lost her son in the war,

says her daughter ran away.

       smell of blood and the
taste of gasoline and the windows
have all been boarded over.

the afternoon is wasted trying to
find a door that still opens.

rest of the day

is burned to the ground.

AND IT'S A LIFE AND IT'S NOT A LIFE AND EVERYONE RESENTS THE IDEA OF HOPE

plug is pulled and
last goodbyes at 2 a.m then
down to the price chopper for a
12-pack, try to convince shelly to
come over when her shift is done but
she says her husband is in town
because she always says her
husband is in town. and we're the
only people in the store, and
we're shouting, trying to be heard
over the 24-hour no repeat boomer
soundtrack that plays to fill the
empty spaces, and it's gordon fucking
lightfoot, okay? wreck of the edmund

fitzgerald, a goddamn history lesson
if you're lucky enough to be
right here, right now, hoping to get
into shelly's pants. and that pedal
steel wailing up and down the
aisles, past the tampons and the
tangerines, past the cocoa fucking
pebbles, and he has to be dead by
now, i'm guessing? not lightfoot, my
father, and shelly says she needs
to get back to stocking shelves, and
i think i finally understand that
the passing days are just a drug to
make you forget about
desperation.
and i realize i've
wasted too much of my life
in this town.

i realize i've wasted too much of
my life being me.

and i pay for the beer
and go home.

POEM, A WEEK LATER

wake up in a stranger's bed on
your 53rd birthday knowing it's
the beginning of the end of your life.

two in the afternoon,
hungover,
all names forgotten.

all pasts absolved

and the present tense is history,
of course, and the future is
nothing worth remembering.

you get there finally, and
everyone you ever loved is
either dead or dying.

THE LAST AGE, WITHOUT APOLOGY

all of us dead at the end of the day,
and some of us stoned.

no religions, no gods, no flags,
but i doubt you have the guts.

i doubt the house survives the fire,
but we can always build it again
from the bones of your children.

we can always drink the blood of priests from
the discarded skulls of politicians, because
the future is a prison,
the past a dream.

bowie, 1974, or manson with his
runaway daughters and his beatles albums:

good times beneath the california sun.

the news of the day spelled out in
blood on every bedroom wall,
and all we ever wanted was
to get laid, you know?

all we ever wanted
was to get rich.

and what else was america ever
going to be but a place for all things
pure & true to go and die?

THE SOUND OF THE TRUTH BEING

TOLD BY A LIAR

and he's tired of his mortality,

yeah,

but so what?

we're all born

dead or dying.

we're all the failures our

parents raised us to be, and he

wants to reach out to his children but

his hands have been cut off at the elbows.

he wants to sing them lullabies,

but his tongue has been torn out.

the government?

sure—

all pain should be
someone else's fault.

all gods should be rounded up
like stray dogs and shot.

just takes that first small
taste of blood and you're hooked.

POEM FOR A NEW RELIGION

there is nothing more
easy for a coward to hate than
a man who has no use for god.

there is no god i would
ever believe in more than
i believe in the woman i love.

this is how beauty
spreads out its roots
       and grows.

HEX

feels so fucking right caught in the
undertow at the edge of town,
eyes closed against the copper sky and dreaming.
sweating god's blood into weed-filled back yards,
into the weed-filled parking lots of abandoned
shopping plazas.
and from here there is only the interstate
to take you to more of what you've left behind.

from here it is only 10,000 miles to the
sacred shrine of st maria,

to the ghost of beth made flesh.

and i remember her smile and
the feeling of holiness and
i remember waves of pure sunlight.

i remember being someone better.

i forget why i

thought it would ever matter.

AND I REMEMBER I AM WITH YOU
WHEN I DIE

there is nothing radical and
there is nothing,

there is nothing in between.

there is everything
        left behind

              good?

              sure.

and these whores so
desperate for power don't
want your faith, don't want your soul,

they just want you on
your knees.

these ideas of strength that
only use domination as a yardstick and
that there is nothing
less than zero.

that there is both a
straight line and a brick wall—

not a riddle
but a fact,

a challenge.

man breaks the slave's legs
and then tells him to run,

woman drops the baby down the well.

and remember that there is
only room for victors in
this age of plenty.

there are reasons to live but
only for those who know the secret,

only for those who have
hoarded the wealth
and the power.

if there's no one left to say
stop!
they can just
go on killing forever.

or early autumn beneath the
luminous weight of max ernst skies,

narcotic sunlight haze and the
almost-silence of static and hum

your life
which is a given.

your death will never
make any sense.

each poem and each poem and
each poem and that they
celebrate fear,

that they understand joy.

that there is

always

one less to write.

IN THE LESSER WORLD

this wasteland of our own invention,

these junkies gnaw on
the bones of angels.

thought i told you i loved you when
we were both 16, but i was wrong.

thought the desert
would have boundaries,

thought escape would
always be an option.

blamed myself for
being so goddamn young

ONE FOR THE MINOTAUR'S WIFE

judas portrayed in faded peeling paint on
the side of a barn or *CHRIST IS THE ANSWER* in
letters 10 feet tall on the side of the hill as
we drive into town:

take one and
to hell with the other.

live quietly on the edge of autumn with a
man who drowned his infant daughter 30 years ago.

sit in the shade of an apple tree while he
nails himself to a cross made from all of the
pain and misery he's ever caused.

give him the truth about god if
that's the kind of person he is,

won't do him any good

but it never hurts to know.

[SO LUCKY, WALKING IN THESE SHOES]

in this sunlit field
full of severed hands:

no justice,

no forward motion.

and crow laughs at your pain and
promises to tell you where
he's hidden the pills, but he lies.

america, right?

sure.

the late summer desert of

upstate new york

and all those missing teenage girls:

the ones you never see again,

the ones who get elected,

the ones who live just long enough to

dig their own shallow graves,

because what's a world without internet porn?

you'll never know

and these are not my rules, okay?

i just lock all the doors and

sit on the bathroom floor in my

burning house.

fear as a way of life,

depression and impotent rage.

and what i think is that i'm always seven,

always on my knees in the wooded lot

out past the playground,

blood and snot running down my face and

the matthews kid from down the

street has a knife, has his pants down,

says just do it, you fucking faggot, and

how do you grow up after this?

you don't.

you mark time and then you grow old,

you get married & divorced.

you forget, but not
in any meaningful way.

pick at the surface and
there's the pus.

nothing heals,

no one forgives.

and crow knows this, sure,
and maybe he looks like my father.

maybe he sounds like my son.

and it's never too late to
ask for kindness, and
it's never too late to offer it, but it's
sure as shit too late to be any better

than the people we've become.

it's a field of severed hands on the
outskirts of whatever dying town
you've spent your life trying to escape.

it's early spring, and
the war refuses to end.

and haven't i been
hearing this same tired refrain
my whole sorry life?

POEM FOR DRINKING THE BLOOD OF THOSE WHO WOULD FIGHT TO KEEP YOU DOWN

in the age of fear,
be the enemy of tyrants;

in the age of ignorance,
believe only in truth.

fuck the addicts and the
whores who
sell their asses for power.

fuck the kings of pestilence and
the queens of disease,
and fuck all of their sycophants—

every castle can be
burned to the ground.

every flag is meaningless:

use them for wrapping corpses,
for wiping your ass.

believe in the
sovereignty of one

pledge allegiance
only to trust

in such obvious ways,
change the world.

AND I CAN SEE WHY YOU MIGHT WANT TO DIE, AND I'M NOT HERE TO SAVE YOU

Early spring, okay? driving north on
the pennsylvania turnpike in the first wave of traffic
hoping to get a good seat for the solar
eclipse, and we get a Doors song on the radio,
something else by Crosbystillsnashandneil and
then Freebird, because why the fuck not? before
the deejay steps up to the mic and shouts with
terrifying orgasmic glee about the
NIRVANA WEEKEND we're in the middle
of, and it's been 30 years now since that
stupid fuck blew his brains out, which means
my father's been dead for 28, never knew his
grandsons because he was a selfish cunt.
and so here they are at 26 and 21, watching

me recede, watching me get smaller,
watching me bleach out like bones left in
the sun until all that's left are these ratty
notebooks filled with all these pointless
ideas that i thought might end up having
some deeper meaning but, christ, was i wrong.

Fuck, was I deluded.

One more far-sighted asshole
jumping into the deep end without
ever learning how to swim.

[I REALLY DIDN'T LOSE YOU, I JUST LOST IT FOR A WHILE]

suicide at 53 and then
back to work the next day, and
is this how you remember it?

end of november like
summer never happened.

rest of your life the same
dead end as anyone else's.

feels pretty good just to
be alive
but maybe not enough.

WE FALL APART

grab the knife by the blade like
your father showed you and
then he tells you you're a disappointment
when all you do is bleed.

he puts his drink down and dies
but he doesn't stop talking,

doesn't stop telling you
what a failure
you've turned out to be.

NOT THE TRUTH, BUT EDGING

CLOSER

man next to you on the
train has his piece of the one true cross,

has his flag and
    his gun and if he wants you dead,
                    you're dead.

if he has a reason,
it will be based on hatred and fear.

all forms of mindless slaughter
can only thrive in a world so
overrun with gods.

[HELL IS YOUR BELIEF]

spent too many years
confusing hope and fear.

walking backwards into burning houses.

a first wife who disappeared
and then a second.

children,

lovers,

drugs, sure, but i don't
remember them ever doing shit.

don't remember a day where the
idea of suicide didn't

cross my mind at some point, and which

choice is it that makes you a coward?

how many strikes does the

prophet get

before we shoot that fucker dead?

any number divided by zero is

the best answer you're gonna get,

and believe in christ, sure, but

just don't waste your entire life

waiting for him to save you.

understand that there are better

things to do on your knees than pray.

any god worth believing in

will tell you the same.

PALL

bravery of indifference,

of remaining motionless,

of sinking.

no one to blame but the
children who
no longer speak to you.

no faith in archaic religions—

the story is liquid.

not eternal, but
eternally shifting.

the decision is made to

raze the concentration camps

& put up memorials instead

or maybe shopping malls

or strip clubs.

progress is

the important thing,

ginsberg is dead and

burroughs doesn't care.

the starving can be

fed oil & asphalt

vegetables from the

fields of chernobyl.

i wanted to be a musician,
you see, but couldn't
stand the idea of having
to learn how to play
an instrument.

wanted to be an artist,
but had no original ideas,
no real talent.

learned that poetry is
what you write when you
have nothing to say.

ask bukowski,

ask all the ones who
kiss his tired ass.

the oceans keep changing
the shape of the land.

prisons are a fact of life:

you can scream and
you can weep and
nothing's going to change.

jesus won't come
crawling back.

stand perfectly still in the
middle of the burning
house and think about this,

think about everything
you've ever bought
because you couldn't

live without it.

any situation can be
funny if you're
far enough removed.

A ROOM OF TRUTHS, A HOUSE OF
RAGE

dead man will fuck you hard,

will ride god's flaming stallion over the

corpses of your children and call it justice and

if the landscape can only be painted with blood then

there are decisions to be made.

there are junkies to crucify and

politicians to hang for the tentative

promise of a brighter tomorrow.

there is a nation of victims just waiting to

blame you for their problems but

screw that.

draw strength from their misery and learn to
drink the marrow from their bones.

understand yourself to be the enemy

and laugh.

STARVING DOG PHILOSOPHY

blood-soaked shroud of christ left

out for the crows, and i will be the silence

that frames these words, if you

will be the fear.

i will let the sky fall down

around us

and call it truth.

will subtract nothing from nothing and

make it my gift to

you and your next lover.

i will make it our future—

a more violent form of beauty if

that's what you want,

or a cause worth killing for.

a song that reminds you of sunlight
on the happiest day of your life.

a ghost
but no one you knew,

no one you've ever loved.

does this narrow it
down at all?

[WILL THE POISON SCAR MY EYES]

and you and i, we were
talking about the
kingdom like true unbelievers.

we were naming the dead,
but not out of love,

not out of necessity.

and is hatred a religion?

look around you,

every possible answer has been
spelled out in the
blood of innocent corpses.

every corpse possesses a
history but no future.

the need for an enemy
is nothing
any of us are born with.

SUMMER '94

says john i might be
dying but at least i'm not a
coward and we're back on
charlotte street here.

we're drunk at two in the afternoon
and i say maybe.

i say maybe and then i pause and
then i say maybe.

i say maybe, but the survivors
are the ones who get to
write history and he laughs

he laughs.

says point for you and
i say maybe.

i say nothing.

sit there with a warm beer in my
hand and wait for a
better way to waste my life.

THE GOOD TIMES ARE HERE TO
STAY

there is no better pain than
the pain we cause others.

there is no better father than
the one we never knew.

are you taking notes?

i'm not just talking for
my health, here.

i'm not telling you anything
you shouldn't already know.

and fuck poetry, right?

right.

life's too short to waste it
speaking in tongues,
whining about injustice,
crawling through the filthy depths of
your own bitter soul.

gimme a 4/4 beat,

gimme shinier lies in
prettier packages.

we'll screw our way through every
assbackwards town in this
bullshit state, and then we'll
move on to the next.

we'll run through
churches, through cemeteries,
through rooms filled with
unwanted children and
listen.

it's a three-legged race
in a pit of quicksand.

it's one last round in
the chamber, and what i
think i need more than anything
is to move somewhere warm.

what i need is to get high
without the phone ringing every
five goddamn minutes, and
how many times do i have
to prove that i will never save anyone?

that no one is

worth saving?

once you start making exceptions,

the future goes up

in flames.

PART II:

the house on fire becomes the palace of ashes

ANGELS AND THE SHADOWS THEY

CAST

or ghosts in the back yard or
a shimmering ring around the sun.

the dead girl still falling but the
ending to her story is already written
and would you kill the ones who
pushed her to this point if you
were given the choice?

fuck
yes.

i am tired of second chances and
i am tired of
fighting cruelty with kindness.

i am sick of upstate
new york in november.

am through with cowardice and with
ignorance passed off as wisdom.

if all of us are forced to bleed
just to be able to play in
someone else's game,
then none of us are going to win.

AND THEN THESE SUNLIT DAYS OF

OBVIOUS JOY

or the song you sing with
your face smashed in,

the blood of christ
collected in a plastic cup—

what matters here is that
love is not an ocean.

the value of human life has
become negligible when set
against the value of oil or
gold and what we consider
are the reasons how.

what we contemplate is why

and there are always more
children to replace the ones
who starve to death to
replace the ones who are
raped who are butchered by
soldiers and by priests and
there is always more wealth
to be stolen and more
wars to be won.

takes some serious fucking
pain to keep you up and
running in the land
of the free.

YOUNG MAN W/ A FUTURE

stand silently in this
sunlit room next to a window with a
view of your past and keep giving
yourself reasons to hate yourself.

slide the knife in low
then pull upwards to the heart.

carefully,

slowly,

the pain's gotta last you
the rest of your life.

THE KINGDOM OF BLOODSTAINED

OBJECTS

some sad drunken asshole hit by a
train in warm october sunlight, some
12 year-old girl jumping to her death from
a water tower,
and i am sorry for all of the pain in the
world but am not above causing
my share of it.

i am beautiful in dark rooms.

i am the sea of static,

an absence of hope but
with it comes
an immunity to pain and, in a

world of addicts and rapists, there is

little room left for the radiant glow

of jesus christ.

these girls on the internet you

jerk off to are all

someone's daughter

whether they want to be or not.

this fear of bloodless gods that

gets passed off as morality is

a joke without a punchline.

all joy enters and

leaves the body through the heart.

all poems are horses

w/ their eyes gouged out,

can't make it any more

obvious than that.

A MURDER AND A MURDER AND A

SUICIDE

dreams of crows in the rain all

blues all greys and

no sound but the sound of breaking hearts.

no houses but houses on fire and

never any homes.

never any reason to visit the graves you

spent so long digging for your parents

because any one truth in this slowly

rusting town is as useless as

all of the others.

any act of deception is better than

no action at all.

twenty years spent like a

blind man trying to paint the sky.

a lifetime of starving dogs weeping

tears of blood for

all the pain they say you've caused them.

are you with me so far?

a teenage girl jumping to her death is

more real than all the gods we've

                        ever invented.

a song of hope is more than we deserve.

a lifetime of pretty words all

crammed down our throats until

we can no longer breathe.

HIDDEN BETWEEN THE BRILLIANT
SKY AND THE DARKENING HILLS

like frightened rabbits in october sunlight, i
kissed you hard up against the shadows
of our fathers' ghosts.

like an act of faith or an uncertain
step onto a narrow ledge
and i remember the walls were blue and
i remember the sky.

remember the angels all
formed a ring around the sun.

the grey-eyed poets and how they
faked their way through such
obvious songs of joy.

pulled back the flesh to expose their beating

hearts for any pretty girl who smiled at them and

there was never any doubt in my mind that

i would tell you that i loved you.

there was never any moment that mattered

more than the one in which we met.

the only truths i accept in these

lost and bitter days are my own.

ARSHILE

powerlines etched into grey sky like
there was never any other reality.

like if you believe in october then you
have no choice but to believe in november and
i was never a big enough fool to accept the
idea of any god who would punish me
for rejecting him.

i was driving to work when i
heard about cobain's suicide but
that was a dozen lifetimes ago.

i had faith in the desert of
my own life then.

was in love with you but you were
married and it would be another 20 years
before we saw each other again.

a lifetime of regrets and
apologies left unspoken or maybe just a
bitter joke told by a desperate junkie.

a small poem written in the
margins of a book i never finished.

all of that time wasted waiting for
just the right moment to die.

INVERTED GRACE

floating in the pale sunlight of early
april, we are not drowning, are not yet
max and dorothea but already something more.

we are believers in
the idea of disbelief.

are casting shadows across ragged lawns and
up the sides of empty houses and
then measuring the distances between
the deaths of our enemies and the deaths of our
friends.

fuck 1967.

all of those junkies who thought your
father was the second coming.

all those teenage girls made of
spun sugar
and we could never eat our fill.

we grew older, of course,
but we never grew up.

learned the hard way that every dog was
only our friend until the moment it wasn't.

spent far too many days bleeding
in the name of what we thought was love.

OR WENDY, WHOSE LAST NAME I NEVER KNEW

and nobody wants the summer of
fun to end, but there's this girl
passed out naked on the bathroom floor.

her sister, laughing in the kitchen,

says to roll her over in case she
pukes, she'll be fine.

says that someone find tony
before he tries to fuck her.

grabs herself a couple of beers
for the road, and she's gone.

[THIS STATE OF GRACE IS CONSUMING ME]

live here without apology without
hope. the plastic bags caught in
the highest branches of dead trees, the
plastic chairs faded in overgrown
november backyards and
what about sunlight?

what about the shadows cast by
houses as they burn from
the inside out?

no love, okay?

no second chances.

we step out into freeway traffic
and the story is over.

one round jacked into
the chamber and, really, what is that
but the true sound of america?

father, sister, mother, the
choice is yours.

the trigger is pulled.

doctor says cancer but
the door is still open.

dog takes a shit and
then eats it.

this will inevitably become

the story of your life.

A CROWN OF BARBED WIRE; A

BLESSING

this man you love,

tell him his whole life doesn't
have to be a premonition of suicide and
does he listen?

does he cry?

everyone's an asshole

anymore.

give him a front seat blowjob out
behind some abandoned factory and then
tell him goodbye.

pull the trigger
while he's sleeping—

even in an ocean of filth,
there are choices.

even after the body is dropped
five stories to the pavement,
the future needs to be considered.

slaves fucking on broken glass,

priests raping children.

everything, everywhere violence and
do you see how
silence becomes a weapon?

a shield?

find me the passage in the bible that

tells the story of

god sniffing after teenage pussy.

let the false king be nailed

to the corpses he creates.

we are all fucked here and

we are all holy and

what then after the last city is completed?

let the fire be all-consuming,

let every clock be

moved back to zero.

the future is only

something you want until

the moment it arrives and then
all you talk about are the simpler
days of the past.

all we become are the people
we've always hated.

they were never anything more
than the whores
we always wanted to be.

BEHIND THE CURTAIN OF ICE

and it's not that i didn't
believe in the slower insanities
because i had known you
for fifteen years and by then,
and it's not that i didn't care.
              but christ,
there was nowhere else to go and
no reason to stay.

five below zero at nine thirty in
the morning, and so
what if the sky was blue?

couldn't get the car to start or
the clocks to run backwards.

could only taste blood in

your kisses, but

kept coming back for more.

BUT YOU CAN'T BE A SAINT TILL
YOU'RE DEAD

it was a moment of truth,
                    a lie,
and it was my life and
                    even now,

                    even here.

year of the plague, kingdom of nil, and
who among us will shoot the pedophile priest?

who will burn down the
corpse-god's castle?

fucker's gonna look good in a shallow grave,

halo of flies and a fistful of lies,

and no one grows fat on a diet of dust.

the thirsty man never chooses a

cupful of sand over a cupful of water,

but what if all choice is removed?

what happens when

tyranny replaces freedom?

it's no small honor to be the enemy of

all these minds warped by

cowardice and fear.

BURNT HILL ROAD, EARLY SPRING

or shooting animals in cages and
laughing
while they bleed to death.

something american.

something to do with your father
on a drunken saturday
afternoon.

to think back on
after your wife has left you.

TREASON

in your house at the end of winter

with the words of christ

spray-painted across every wall.

no love but whatever love can

be found in fucking and

where do the dogs go once they've

licked the blood from our feet?

who buries the orphans

after the war has been lost?

or maybe we burn whatever

we can just to keep warm.

NEWS OF THE MASSACRE REACHES THE KING IN THE SECONDS BEFORE HIS ASSASSINATION

you, in the center of
your labyrinth on the hottest
day of the year.

you,

blinded but not blind,

mouth filled with the sour milk that

pours from your lovers'

open wounds.

you,

without hope or

explanation,

without purpose.

feels so good, but at
some point you have to
start breathing again.

AN UNFINISHED POEM

first day of summer and you are either the
minotaur or the maze and
either way
all hope is lost.

don't feel bad,

don't bleed just because
your father bled.

make a list of everything
that's your fault,

bury it in the narrow space between
your house and house next door.

old woman at the window watches you like a

game show or an execution.

dog barks closer down

towards the river.

sweat now at your hairline and

pooling in the small of your back.

soil is damp here,

never any direct sunlight, always

too much rain.

always the sound of van

morrison in the back of your mind.

maybe madame george maybe

slim slow slider.

not the death of someone you used to
love, of someone you still do, but maybe
their painful retreat from your life until all you
have is the memory of face or a touch,
the taste of salty sweat on bare flesh.

and i recognize you,
of course,
because of the mask you wear.

i understand that all hands are
cages and all words, lies.

am watching a child playing at the
edge of the road and
then i'm watching the empty space where
he used to be.

feels like the sound of a shovel

sinking deep and

striking sudden bone.

THE BEGGAR, WITH HIS HANDS CUT

OFF

in the sunlight taking
pictures of falling water.

in the moment
worried about the future
and denying the past
and none of us born with the
knowledge that all words
are just empty gestures.

the answers to every question
about worth and about
value given only in
terms of money.

the failure that comes from
having none of it.

children at the front door
with eyes full of hope and
empty hands or the ones
left dying in the street.

man with a gun aims it at
your heart, says to help them and
he'll shoot;

is saving just one any
better than
saving none at all?

has the sky ever been so
perfectly blue as it was on
the last day of your life?

it's not the absence of joy or

the absence of beauty that

brings you here, but

the abundance,

the transience.

the knowledge that you have

thrown away more

than you will ever get back.

YOUR GOD, THE PORNOGRAPHER

this false king,
this terminal shitstain

understands the alchemy of
innocent life into death.

gets off on the fine art of
growing fat off the
flesh of corpses, and baby says
she'll make that first shot count.

says she's loved me
since the day we met.

the future unwritten but so
blindingly beautiful she can
only pull me closer

and cry.

UPSTATE SONG

drags his lover
over barbed-wire,
through fields of
thorns, tells her
that god is
always smiling.

says every
sainted martyr
is just tossed aside
    and forgotten in
            the end.

JEFFERS

in the wreckage of your house and in
the wreckage of your life,
all history is the history of failure.

rain for four days until it has
nowhere to go but your basement.

prayers that mean nothing—

gods who bear you
only ill will.

those who are indifferent

choose this path maybe
instead of following leaders who
would rape your children or

the ones who would butcher them
for profit and for glory.

listen carefully to the
sound of the next storm approaching.

move past anger and
into vengeance.

no wrongs have ever been
righted by hands
wrapped tight around emptiness.

AND LAUGHTER AND MEANINGLESS

JOY

the storm and then the
silence before the storm that follows.

pale yellow skies over car crashes
and prayers and the
steady buzz of insects.

the river
where your son took his life,

the hills repeating themselves
endlessly in all directions.

you get tired of being told
what to do but so what?

your choices come down to a
diet of bitter shit or a
diet of starvation, and even these
are offered grudgingly.

and so you live or you
die and the world keeps
crawling forward.

the house on fire
becomes
the palace of ashes.

call it home,

dig your grave.

you have a long life ahead
of you still, but

it's best to be prepared.

late summer suicide,

and if you know nothing then
there is nothing worth knowing.

does this sound like
something your father taught you,
or were those your mother's words?

or what if all she said was
you know nothing?

what if all she meant was that
you are nothing?

seems like you could always
taste this in the back of

your throat.

MY FATHER, IN THE GREY YEARS

seems a little quieter after
the first suicide, right?

seems a little smaller, like we're
always seeing him from a distance.

like the bones were already
broken when we got here,
and what we're doing now is
just waiting for him to choke on them.

what we're doing now is
something
between murder and mercy killing

and i promise not to stop
if you don't.

YOU BELIEVE IN THE FUTURE,

DON'T YOU?

good little piggy on
his hands and knees,
mouthful of shit and
no reason to be
left alive.

just get him once
between his blind and
hate-filled eyes and
we'll call it
a mercy killing.

[A HELL OF A PRICE FOR YOU TO GET YOUR KICKS]

dead man tells you self-hatred isn't a gift,
isn't a talent,
but he's probably wrong.

fucker killed his lover
then forgave himself.

says he's spoken to god
but won't say about what,

won't tell you where he
scored the acid.

and he says he used a knife,
just in case you were wondering,

just in case you were taking notes.

finished the job as quickly as
he could,
then turned the blade on himself.

NO END TO HAPPINESS

hang out with whoever
has the dope,
maybe a handjob or
some finger-fucking,
maybe a quick lay
on the bathroom
floor.

an overdose in
the tub,

get up in
the morning and
start looking
to score.

[I KNOW WHAT YOU WANT AND I
SEE WHAT YOU SEE]

and none of these lies are going to kill you,
but the idea of suicide
always confuses the situation.

how much is your life worth,
and how much are you owed?

and if everyone saw hope,
we'd have a future,
but then where would the government be?

fucked,
just like rest of us,
and if j christ could have only been
a better dog, we wouldn't have had to

gouged the bastard's eyes out

if cobain wasn't such a pussy,
he'd be a middle-aged junkie by now.

wouldn't have anything
too important to say, but then he
never really did.

[A RIDE TO THE OPEN GATES]

and everyone says
you're gonna die
but everyone's a liar.

everyone's a minor god,
       a junkie,
       a failed prophet,
and are your parents
gone for the weekend?

good.

getting too
goddamn cold to keep
partying down at the
softball field.

getting too old to keep
hitting on these
high school kids.

you buy them beer,
you give them ecstasy,
but then you've got to talk
to them once you're through
                    fucking.

gotta smile,
gotta laugh,
gotta pretend to
give a shit.

reassure them they're
never gonna die.

doesn't really cost a thing,

but it's still more

than i'm willing to pay.

[SCRAMBLING LIKE DOGS FOR A
SHARE]

blonde girl says she's 17,
so why not believe her?

got three more hours to kill
before work, and no weed,

no more vodka in the freezer.

gotta grab whatever
good times you can find.

[THERE'S NO DOUBT OF THE
FUTURE IN MY HEAD]

too much of each day wasted
thinking about suicide & murder,
about assassination,
when all i really want to do is sleep.

wake up in the
morning and leave,

get as far away from
all of you as possible.

[A PRIMAL TRUTH AS PURE AS ICE]

six years old, maybe seven,

friday night in the corner of your living room,

in your red dinosaur pajamas,

pushing hot wheels around a group of potted plants

and

the babysitter's name is annie and she's laughing and

her boyfriend is here,

stopped over to surprise her,

brought a few friends,

a few cases of beer, some pot, some albums

and your parents won't be back until sunday.

your bedtime isn't until you fall asleep,

and its *faeries wear boots* up loud enough to

make the speakers shake,

and you smile to yourself when you hear

someone mention the name of the song,

and are you a little high?

probably.

and one of the boyfriend's friends
keeps handing you his beer,
and it tastes awful and you keep taking small sips
because it makes him laugh.

because happiness is a drug

and it takes you another 30 years to realize
things were never this good again.

IN THE GARDEN OF DYING STARS

or junkie truth,

which is not the truth—

a victim's idea of power.

grey sun in a grey sky

and this old man sleeping in his

hospital bed looks like me,

                   like my father,

like the spaces that grow between us,

and hope matters,

          of course,

but let's not screw around here,

the false king is a dead man.

the poet without a gun
really has nothing to offer.

and i remember telling you this on
the day before your lover's suicide,
and i remember all of the reasons
you gave for hating me.

i remember silence.

young boy crying in the middle of
main street, and
then the scream of brakes.

only a small loss,
                right?

gotta look at the bigger picture,

gotta build better bombs.

the poor can take care of themselves,
and tough shit if they can't.

no one starves in
a nation of corpses.

no one needs god
when a holy man can
fuck them just as good.

understand this, and you might
just turn out okay.

PART III:

how much of your pointless pain

are you willing to blame on everyone else?

SISTER

dog on fire says nothing, and
the words are mistaken
for love

little hands,
little fingers, tiny bones,
and you will suck the marrow
                    from each one

you will feed the
ashes to your lover

feels good to be
a part of something bigger

LOSS RECOVERY

a believer in nothing from
nothing, he is shot dead by
those he put his faith in.

he is the sound of laughter,

he is a feast for the crows.

end of december and still no
snow, and once you get to the
top of echo hill you have
nowhere to go but down.

and think about dali in
his bed of flames,

think about gorky.

set that fucker's suicide to

a 4/4 beat and

i guarantee you a hit because,

at the end of the day,

everybody just wants to dance.

at the end of the war,

everyone is ready for another.

feels so good to kill, why

would you ever want

to stop?

[ALL THE YOUNG MEN SING LIKE BLACKBIRDS AND THRUSHES]

and in this world of assholes,
all the girlfriends are bleeding,

all the drummers are suicides,
all the guitarists, overdoses,
and none of the albums sell.

none of the plans for the future
ever come to fruition.

everyone swears they're
getting clean
right after the party,
but everyone lies.

everyone smiles.

everyone staggers home
to fall down and die.

WHAT THE FUTURE TASTED LIKE,

AND WHY WE SWALLOWED IT

told her you were always my
favorite war but then i grew up,

then i got tired of bleeding.

and she laughed, told me about
her mother's boyfriend,
about the living room and the
bedroom and the bathroom floor and
it was 1989 and it was 1992.

blowjobs in the church parking lot,

boy found in the river.

drove out to buffalo listening

to merrittville on the tape player,

shooting up like iggy, and he

told her this is where your life begins.

and she told me none of this

will mean anything five years from.

now and i believed her

gave her the reds and i gave her

the blues and

it was the end of november.

told her this is the end

and she smiled,

closed her eyes then stepped on the gas.

said 3rd day of the 3rd month and
it was her brother's O.D. we
were talking about.

it was the simple fact of
being bigger than christ.

of coming out of orbit and crashing
hard into some barren
upstate field.

fucking kid toking up in the
basement next door,

his girlfriend puking
on the back steps.

never knew who pulled the
trigger, never cared.

house burned down with only the
baby inside and she opens her eyes.

says she misses her sister,

couldn't care less about her father.

sent her a postcard from the sea of
cortez 5 or 6 years ago and
then nothing and then she laughs.

pulls over to the edge of the highway,

tells me i was never the truth and
then she drives away.

[NEVER AGAIN, NEVER AGAIN,

NEVER AGAIN]

and so the

suicide's son

grows up to

be a suicide,

and the dogs

are still hungry.

no hope,

really,

for any of us

cowards &

addicts in

this age of fear.

no compassion

in this land of

one-sided laws and

moneyed whores.

just bury

the fucker and

wait for

whoever's

next.

ONE FROM THE AGE OF SUBTLE
ATROCITIES

living close to water
and without fear,

living alone with the
wife and the secrets.

small failures mean nothing
in windowless rooms,
small victories even less.

look

it isn't a story,
but an idea.

man locks his daughter in
the basement when she's
18 and then keeps her there
for 24 years.

rapes her,

fathers her children,

signs deals for the movie,
            the sequel,
            the video game.

considers god like you
would a second helping
of dessert.

considers dessert

all of these choices to

be made while the crows

gather outside his

      door.

IN THE SHADOW OF ST.

ATHANASIUS

down fairmont to argonne then
through the drainage tunnel that runs beneath
the freeway and
how much time did we waste
crying over cobain's death?

how much of yr pointless pain are
you willing to blame on everyone else?

some sad little loser giving blowjobs in
the scrub brush down by the river.

some stupid goddamn war fought
in the name of
preserving peace for the survivors.

kid was lying there bleeding in
the e-z mart parking lot but
he said he was fine.

said he just needed a cigarette and we
were driving out to mooresville.

we were looking for your sister,

said she still owed you $50 or at
least some weed.

at least a little crank but
when we got there
the trailer park was gone.

when i was through growing up
i just started growing old.

thought about how the asshole wanted to

die, so what were we upset about?

thought about what a waste my

life was, and then she called two

months later to say she'd finally found the bitch.

told her my car was in the shop and she

told me i'd always been a crappy liar.

told me she's found someone else and

i remember daydream nation

playing in the background.

i remember walking out into sunlight

surrounded by the stench of decay

and the smothering weight of the future.

the ease with which i forgot

that i'd ever loved you,

the neverending tearstained joy.

ONE FOR THAT FUCKING

TEENYBOPPER, RIMBAUD

sunday morning drawing
x's on the baby's eyes and we'll
say it's the end of something,
okay?

an age or a moment or a century,
so let's be sad.

let's ask the kid's dad if he
has any hash because
what is time, if not time to waste?

don't answer that
just yet.

and you know what we need?

a comprehensive list of poets who
never ended world hunger,

of artists who changed the
course of human events.

more monuments to futility.

more mass graves for the
corpses of assassinated politicians
& world leaders, and it doesn't
matter what you say, the
baby's still a goner.

the pills don't work,

the party runs late.

midnight, then one, then two,

everyone shouting to be

heard over horses on the stereo.

everyone screaming against the

constant howl of gunfire.

doesn't matter which version

of the future you voted for,

all you ever get in

the end is war.

A SEASON OF MINOR GRACE

married to either a junkie or
some minor prophet, summer of '94,
three weeks of nothing but rain and when you
finally called i was still trying to
forget you.

when you were talking about your father's
suicide, i had my hands up your shirt.

no drugs and no booze and the
curtains drawn against the sun.

your brother's house at the far end of
charlotte street where it's only either the
buzz of cicadas or the steady pulse of passing trains.

where the future is always spelled out in
lower case letters on dusty mirrors,

not i love you but fuck me.

not joy but a temporary
obliteration of pain—

it's all i can offer
because it's all we deserve.

CLEAN, UNPROMISED AND
OBSCENE

dog is sick and so
beat it to death.

hang it from the tallest
tree down on the riverbank.

nothing but choices right?

cast your vote or
pull the trigger.

get on your knees,

one of them has his
hands down your pants,

tells you to say *i'm a faggot*,
other one keeps screaming he
fucked your sister, keeps saying
she begged for more, and
how the hell did we
end up here?

how old were you when
jeannie swallowed the poison?

can't care about everything,
i guess?

can't remember the
ending to every story, but it
seems like someone would have
ended up getting sucked off,
or at least beaten and
pissed on.

at least a broken arm.

and it seems like a new
president would've been elected,
a new war declared, and what were
any of us ever going to grow up
to be other than afraid?

what are we going to fear
if not everything?

who's going to end up paying
for our pain if not the world?

[IT'S NEVER TOO LATE, BUT IT STILL
AIN'T ANY USE]

christ or manson,
right?

fuck yes,

just ask pettibon.

rock & roll and fifteen year-old groupies and
all of us singing HELTER SKELTER
while the nails are driven home—

good times in the american desert,

good sex on the bathroom floor.

and show me a man who
isn't afraid to die and i'll stand back
while you pull the trigger.

a cup of sand or
a cup of blood,
and which one will you choose?

every question is a trick question,

every bridge is just waiting for
the right moment to collapse.

and so you've got the gun and
so you've got a plan.

you've seen the movie and
memorized the songs.

first shot gets the

false prophet in the throat, right?

feels like god or like

fucking his wife.

that good,

but what if

truth is never truth until

it actually happens,

the priests rape your children and

all you can think to do is pray

eyes wide open and totally blind and

this is why every kingdom is

the kingdom of nil.

this is why we have always been

our own greatest failure—

all pain matters, but only until

the moment it passes.

EVERY WORTHLESS DAY IN THE

SEASON OF RAIN

so you and i, we talk about
the deaths of minor gods.

talk about Eliot, about poetry, about
how it can only ever be a curtain,
something used to cover or reveal the truth of the sun,
and then the sun itself, yellow or dull silver
or luminous white.

grey shadows on dead grass—

the spaces between houses,
       between cities,
       between lovers.

you and i on either side.

the exile of hope
in the age of ignorance.

walls and windows and distance and fear, and
what will we do when there's nothing left
to eat but the past?

how much blood will it take
to quench your thirst?

it's not just a question asked
out of idle curiosity.

THE REAL STORY

baby always looks her best
in the burning house.

says she's not afraid of death but
i don't know what that means.

i have stood next to my father's corpse
in an unlit hospital room at
1:30 in the morning.

i have crawled down antiseptic
hallways choked with
stuttering fluorescent lights only to end up
more lost than when i began.

smell of weeds and damp rot
and a mouthful of dirt.

sneaker pressed firmly against the
back of my neck and my pants
around my ankles, and do we build our
lives out of the parts we choose
to remember?

are the drugs you buy now any
better than the ones you
bought in high school?

and baby laughs,
says, "of course they are", and
the flames are snaking up her arms.

tells me she loves me, but
this isn't where i belong.

pewter blue skies over

flowering trees, over power lines and

dead-end streets and i am

afraid to stay in one place too long.

i am afraid to move.

we are none of us safe from

harm until

the moment we die.

MIXED MEDIA, METAL ON METAL

most of his life spent waiting for
rain in a sinking house,

funny shit.

a deep belief in fear and an
unending fear of death.

the simple grace of a small
backyard filled with flowers.

magdalena with her torn and
tortured wings,

tell her you'll love her if she'll
walk into the sea.

tell her that her

husband's assassination was

inevitable.

this is the new world—

i am the sun in human form.

am an argument for the

sainthood of lester Bangs or at

least of debbie harry and

what if time refuses to

stop in 1978?

21st goddamn century

happens with no premonition.

sweetheart fucked and high

all summer long, lying naked on

the bathroom floor.

crawling through warm fields of
sunflowers, face and knees
all cut and bleeding, throat bitten
by christ's sharpened teeth and
she said her husband was
gone again.

says her boyfriend
just doesn't get it.

has empty hands and a
mouthful of someone else's poems—

not wisdom,
just words.

taste of stale faith and wasted
lives and do you remember
pollock laughing as the car
slammed into the tree?

explain why the joke is
funny, and it's ruined.

set the church on fire,

place the gun
against the child's head.

doesn't take much strength to
survive in a coward's world

[I DREAM AS YOU CAN DREAM]

1973 and the
neighbor's house on fire.

the babysitter stoned and
her boyfriend laughing.

has his hand down her shorts,
tells you to turn the stereo up.

tells you to get him
another beer out of the fridge,
and the sound of sirens
in the distance.

the future not here yet,
but fucking unstoppable

just killing everything
in its path.

NOTHING EASIER TO MAKE THAN AN ENEMY

friday night outside the
dead man's infirmary, this kid on
fire in the middle of the road,
her father drunk,
his mother stoned,
and so we keep killing god.

we keep dreaming the
assassinations of
politicians.

keep buying more guns for the
arrival of the inevitable.

only things you can ever
end up being in this world
are for or against.

SLEEPING GAS

in the distance in the pale grey

                    sunlight,

dust on your hands

in your mouth and

the highways where the cities end

the spaces between them all.

broken glass and brown grass,

all emptiness and pain moving

towards the hills

dreaming of franco of pollock.

of picasso and the small

moments he invented

the women he buried

and there is no turning away

here in the first bitter days of

                    february.

there is no cause for joy,

no forest that is not on fire.

and in the distance there are

horses.

there are riders

there are fighter planes

coming in low,

casting shadows over

everything we have yet to build.

ALWAYS APPROACHING LOST

a nation of assholes with guns
hoping for someone to shoot.

a suicide's last hit song
on the radio.

end of winter, probably, and the
earth scraped raw,
and where do we go now?

the past has been wasted,
the future will get its turn.

do you need this is writing?

1968, 1998, 2018,
doesn't really matter

dead man on the balcony,

empty faces in the crowd, and

people will always tell you that

hope is a choice but just

saying it doesn't make it true.

just being alive doesn't

make what you have a life.

i'm thinking of myself here,

but i know i'm not alone.

JANE

camera follows the car and then
the car loses control and
then just empty road.

music which is possibly
only in my head.

the laughter of children at the
idea of dead cops, because hatred
is so easy to learn.

you fuck the bull
and then you build the maze.

god chooses favorites, who lives,
who dies, who makes the laws
that control the lives of

the powerless.

wait for spring, then,

the ice will break
and the bodies will surface.

the dog chained to a
tree and then forgotten;

no, not forgotten,
just abandoned.

take this literally or use it as a
metaphor, and who fucking cares?

the camera follows the car, you
see, and then there's a gunshot

a spiderwebbed windshield.

the driver slumping
out of sight.

this sorry little illusion that
motion equals accomplishment.

ERIE STREET IN THE WRONG YEAR

pewter blue sky above the blossoming trees,

above the powerlines,

the slowly collapsing houses.

call it home if you want,

but still dream of escape.

still wait for the news of your father's death,

of your lover's suicide, of the

bombs as they hit the sleeping village.

shit happens, of course, and no one's

gonna hold still

while you try to pin the blame on them.

no one's gonna force you to

suck the marrow from the bones of j christ,

but it's something to think about.

and the age of silver was always a lie,

and morrison had that voice,
but his poetry was shit.

woman i knew swore her baby was his,
but this was in '92 and her
boyfriend kept stopping by work to
tell me i was a dead man, and so
i learned how to become invisible.
i turned crawling into an artform and,
when i saw her again five years later,
most of her teeth were gone.

no light in her eyes, no laughter, and
when i asked how the kid was doing, she
didn't know what i was talking about.

said her wings had been clipped,

said her head was
wreathed in flames.

asked me to kiss her, but i was
already sliding into the future.

MESSAGE TO THE GOOD THIEF,

WHO DIED FOR NO ONE'S SINS

we dig deeper into emptiness,

we call it belief—

not poems, but weapons,

              walls.

a fortress built from
de chirico's bones, from their shadows.
and what i'm sorry for is the timing,

always too late.

the rooms of my childhood
thick with dust.

the weight of our failures
used against us.

live your whole life pressed
flat to the ground,
without ever knowing you have wings.

let the phone ring and
the house burn.

all gods are whores,
all politicians, cancer.

10,000 years of killing is a start,
but then what?

your enemy's enemy,

your lover's lover,

and a corpse is
a corpse, of course.

you fuck or you're fucked and,
either way,
the goal is survival—
these endless days of giving.

here in the first unforgiving
heat of summer with the dogs all
tearing at the corpse of christ.

feels good,
licking yr lover's wounds.

feels better watching her
rip them open.

says she needs a ride to
teri's house but the car keys
                    are missing.

tells you you're an asshole.

asks how many times
you've fucked her sister.

gives you time to come up
with the answer
that'll hurt her most.

THE PLAN

saved ammunition massacred the
prisoners with hoes with machetes then
smashed the children's skulls the babies'
skulls against tree trunks so there'd be
no witnesses no protests no one to
grow up and avenge the murders of
their parents and it was early spring and
it was the end of summer was the dead
of winter. it was past tense once it was
over until it happened again and we
were outraged and we were nameless
and we were victorious.

we were the holy fucking gospel spit
straight from the mouth of god.

LOVE SONG FOR THE BETRAYED

all of us here in
this room without oxygen,
waiting to be forgiven and it seems
like the safest place.

feels like the fist of god
punching a million starving children in
the throat, and you know the
fucker's laughing or else why would he
let them starve in the first place?

seems like the laziest of wasting all
that time inventing religions
instead of looking for solutions.

seems like a world full of inbred
assholes with shit

spilling from their open mouths.

JUL 25TH

or a world filled with

objects just waiting to be bought

or dead houses placed

against a flat landscape.

silence on the verge of being

raped by the mindless

noise of progress.

tv,

radio,

internet and

all of it defined by an

absence of knowledge.

a forest without shadows

and then an ocean of despair.

a fist to the

sleeping child's face.

a nation of wolves,

of whores,

of hopeless suicides

and they will always be happiest when

making money from your pain.

they will always be happy

to cause you more.

SIMULACRA

one more asshole wandering

blind & lost in the desert.

one more starving poet,

one more gracious liar and a

never-ending supply of teenage girls

waiting to be tied up and

fucked in front of

the camera.

feels like we need a war here

or some new group of people to

persecute and crucify—

feels like rain.

silver sky streaked with grey and
these old men hiding behind
locked doors.

these children shooting at cats
& dogs with pellet guns.

shooting each other and laughing and
then the body of someone's runaway
daughter pulled from the river.

been raped, of course, and
you can give her a name and
you can give her a face and still

　　　　　　　　no one cares.

invent new religions to justify
your atrocities and
then invent new atrocities,

build strip malls

between the cemeteries.

parking lots filled with shining chrome,

mouths filled with rust, and this

still the desert,

of course,

and we are all still lost.

words are either

spelled out in neon or

they're meaningless.

no one here will ever

admit to promising you a

future worth inheriting.

POEM BUILT AROUND THE
PHANTOM OBJECT

sunlit afternoon seen from behind
                tinted glass.

silence of the air-conditioning
of clouds over distant hills.

not an absence of hope but
not the presence of it either.

a dull grey emptiness,
            maybe.

the death of christ
which turned out not to
matter at all.

you're here aren't you?

you have your hatreds,
your bitter passions,
your petty jealousies.

you've learned as
little as the rest of us.

know the words to all the
same meaningless songs,
know the pointless punchlines to
all the same unfunny jokes
and do you ever get
tired debating the existence
of any of the gods?

children will starve to death
no matter how

passionately you believe.

some fucker with a gun and a
grudge will always be waiting to
show us just how pissed he is.

just how much innocent blood
the cup of faith can hold.

ABOUT THE AUTHOR

John Sweet sends greetings from the rural wastelands of upstate NY. He is a firm believer in writing as catharsis, and is generally opposed to organized religions and political ideologies. His writing is an amalgamation of abstract art, Surrealism, post-punk and casual rage. He has been publishing in the small press for 30 years. Among his collections are *Bastard Faith*, *No One Starves to Death in a Nation of Corpses* and *Not Everything is About You.*

www.ingramcontent.com/pod-product-compliance
Lightning Source LLC
Chambersburg PA
CBHW031508120626
46545CB00005B/1795